FISHING FOR LEVIATHAN

OTHER BOOKS BY RODNEY DECROO

Allegheny, BC
Next Door to the Butcher Shop

FISHING FOR LEVIATHAN

RODNEY DECROO

Anvil Press // Vancouver

Copyright © 2023 by Rodney DeCroo

All rights reserved. No part of this book may be reproduced by any means without the prior written permission of the publisher, with the exception of brief passages in reviews. Any request for photocopying or other reprographic copying of any part of this book must be directed in writing to Access Copyright: The Canadian Copyright Licensing Agency, Sixty-Nine Yonge Street, Suite 1100, Toronto, Ontario, Canada, M5E 1E5.

Library and Archives Canada Cataloguing in Publication information is available upon request.

Cover design: rayola.com
Interior: HeimatHouse
Represented in Canada by Publishers Group Canada
Distributed by Raincoast Books

The publisher gratefully acknowledges the financial assistance of the Canada Council for the Arts, the Government of Canada and the Province of British Columbia through the B.C. Arts Council and the Book Publishing Tax Credit.

Anvil Press Publishers Inc.
P.O. Box 3008, Station Terminal
Vancouver, B.C. V6B 3X5 CANADA
www.anvilpress.com

PRINTED AND BOUND IN CANADA

Dedicated to Russell Thornton

For helping me
stand up to myself
and to write
better poems.

Special Thanks to:

Rachel Humphries and the staff
At Moniack Mhor Writers Centre
in Scotland for treating me so kindly
during my residency. Several of these poems
were written there in my little room overlooking
the valley. Scottish poet Claire Askew
for tolerating my fanboy gushes
and novelist Juliette Forrest
for her friendship.

"Canst thou draw out Leviathan with a fish hook?
Or press down his tongue with a cord?"
— Job 40:25

TABLE OF CONTENTS

I

Mid-Atlantic Diction and a Nightmare Sow—13
Going into Winter—14
Veterans Day—15
Encounter with an Ostrich—16
Fishing for Leviathan—17
The Burning Horses of Uncle Jack's Eyes—20
That Day in America—23
Serpent and I—25
Coward—26
Mr. Gustafson—27
Why I'm not a Nature Poet—28
The Buck—29
Ghosts—30
Language—31
Soul Mates—32
Strippers—33
Salt—35
Beaufort, South Carolina—36
Gimpy—37
That Fly Lays Eggs—39
Strange Bird—40
Love—41
There Is Something in the Tree—42
Perfect—43
Poetry Is Everywhere—44
Almost Summer—45

II

A Girl from Kansas City—49
Shooting Stars—51
Six Bottles of Wine—52

The Prophet—53
The Sick Buffalo—55
I Don't Date Drunks—57
My Self-Pity Is Bigger than Yours—58
Always True—59
The Podium—60
Steve Dabrowski—61
Your Eyes—62
The Bar—63
What the Dead Hear—64
Booms and Busts—65
Postcards—66
Reading Frost—67
This Building Talks to Me—68
A Political Poem—69
Frozen Cherries—70
Warmed in the Vacuum of Space—71
Tying the Centuries Together like a Funeral Wreath—72

III

Human Traces—75
The Caterpillar—76
I Knew a Songwriter—77
You Wanted to Be—78
The Luthier—79
Poor Man's Doves—80
I Met Death in the Cereal Aisle—81
A Confessional Poem—82
My Therapist Tells Me—84
The Writers Festival—86
Moniack Mhor—87
Learning to Ride—89
Mistatim—90
Safeway—92
Isolation—93

Leftovers—95
Poetry Class—96
Not Ready—97
Flash Grenades—98
A Winter's Moon—99
Dirty Snow—100
A Whole Lot of Nothing—101
Tara—102
PTSD-103
A Thin Thread of Light—104
Brazilian Jiu Jitsu—107
Blue Apartment—109
Stop Being Old—110
The Hug—112

I

Mid-Atlantic Diction and a Nightmare Sow

At theatre school they tried to correct
my posture and make my diction soft.
But I was a razor wrapped in black velvet
soaked in possum's blood. A hamlet
was three abandoned miners' houses
on the opposite bank of the Allegheny River
where a nightmare sow rooted in the polluted earth.
I ain't got nothing against a mid-Atlantic accent,
but there's a poisoned hill with a gut-shot deer,
an incestuous killer and a young boy
with bruised raspberries for eyes. I need
to set it all adrift on a flaming barge.
I need to see the whole shitshow
lit up like a burning Ferris wheel
on a Friday night in western Pennsylvania.
I'd like to see one last time, young Horatio
selling tickets to the freak show tent
as he pockets half the cash. For heaven
and earth are all for the taking,
and there is so much more
than he imagines.

Going into Winter

My father liked hurting people.
It made him feel powerful.
He beat up drunks and his children.
But he wasn't just a bully,
he was a dangerous man, an ex-marine
who said he enjoyed killing.
He called it going into winter—
a state of emotional detachment
where anything was possible;
where he said a man found himself.
That's why he worked in bars.
There was always someone
willing to fight. In Fort St. John
he chased a man from the bar
of the Condill Hotel into the lobby
beating him with the butt-end
of a sawed-off pool cue
while my brothers and I watched.
Finished, he cleaned the cue
on the man's jacket. My mother
said the war made him that way.
When they dated in high school
he was gentle and funny. One night
after work he came into my room.
He sat on the end of my bed. He
made small sounds like he was crying
or choking. I couldn't see him
in the darkness of the room; just
a darker shape within the blackness—
a shadow slowly becoming a man.

Veterans Day

My father said to me once while drunk
that they made him a Marine at Parris Island.
And a Marine, he said, is a killer.

I knew a lot of killers. I knew them in living rooms,
supermarkets, hardware stores, schools, churches,
taverns and all the regular places. Few had been to prison
except for the cells behind their eyes, where they served
life sentences with dead friends and the enemies
they'd killed. Some taught me to play baseball,
some taught Sunday school, some taught me to fight,
drink, smoke cigarettes or chew snuff, to fish,
hunt, sing and shoot pool. Some showed me gentleness,
the value of silence, to use my mind,
to hate no one. Some taught me to fear people
with dark skin or people who worshipped
different gods. Some beat me or did worse things
I can't talk about. I knew a lot of killers.
They were our fathers, uncles and grandfathers.
They were men who worked the mines, mills,
barges and railroads. They were men who never
spoke to us about the killing they were made
to do. Some were men who left their families
to wander from town to town like wild dogs
shot down by other killers in uniforms outside liquor
stores or to slowly die on bar stools with a drink
in their hand and their names never spoken again
at the family table. I knew a lot of killers. Today
we're asked to remember when all they
want to do is forget.

Encounter with an Ostrich

When I was nine years old
I looked inside the moon.
It was easy. I plucked it from the sky
and broke it across my bony knee
like a fat ostrich egg. A clear goo
streaked with yellow leaked
from its cracks. In the clear substance
was the soul of my entire family.
It was terrifying to hold all this
in my small hands.
Oh no, I thought, I've broken
the moon and god will be angry.
I hid it under my bed.
In the morning it was gone.
The day was longer than a year
and supper lasted a century.
Finally, it was time to go to bed.
I lay beneath my blanket.
In the window was the moon.
The night was a wild
and angry ostrich eye.

Fishing for Leviathan

At the back of Jim's Hardware by rows
of fishing rods, reels and tackle boxes,
Ron watched for the store manager
Mr. Liberati and Debbie the cashier
who mostly smoked, read paperbacks
or tended her nails, while my brothers
and I shoved packages of lead sinkers,
fishing hooks and dough balls
down our pants. Ron bought a spool
of line or steel leaders as we strolled
past the checkout waiting for the shout
to stop as the automatic doors swung open
to let us out to the parking lot.
Clutching rods and tackle boxes,
steering one-handed, we pedalled
our bikes down back streets and across
the tracks, to our secret spot by the Allegheny River.
Alongside the slow flow of the current,
as coal barges slipped past, we sat cross-legged
on concrete slabs tying our hooks to fishing lines,
attaching tear-shaped lead sinkers and clumping balls
of greyish dough around the hooks. Finished, we cast
our clumps of bait beneath the power cables,
our thin lines arcing out and dropping
with a distant splash into the deep waters
of the river. Speaking quietly to each other,
our eyes upon our rods, the tips bent,
lines pulled taut by the pull of the current,
sunlight warm against our faces, the far drone
of the tug boats like a music the river
made that called us back each day,
we waited for the sudden tug and dip

of a line as a fish took the bait. The lucky fisherman
grabbed his pole and jerked it high into the air,
to set the hook into the mouth of the feeding fish.
The rest of us, shouting advice, urged him
on to reel it in, the rod bent with the struggling weight
of the hooked prey, the reel's action whining
as he wound it in, as we scrambled for the net
to scoop the thrashing fish ashore. We stood
around the catfish, tangled in the threads
of net, its mucus-slick, greyish-green
mottled sides pulsing in the suffocating air,
dilated black eyes growing a milky film,
grey whiskers drooping, dirt-covered,
it struggled against the ground.
And though we'd seen a catfish hundreds
of times before, we marvelled at our prize.
Man, he's a big one!
Yeah, sure is an ugly sucker too!
You know, they're as old as dinosaurs.
No way, that's bullshit!
No man, they're super old.
I think it looks like an alien.
No, it looks more like a sea monster;
like the Leviathan Pastor Bob preached about
last Sunday!
Nah, it's way too small.
They say the catfish at the bottom
of the river are seven feet long!
Holy shit, they could eat you.
Oh man, I'd like to catch one of those!
No, you wouldn't. You wouldn't
want nothing to do with one of them!
Silent, we stared at it. I freed it
from the net, sliding a hand downwards
from the bulky head to press the spiky fin

—that easily could stab into your palm—
flat against the back. With the fingers
of my free hand I felt for the metal
inside the croaking mouth to gently pry
the barbs loose until the hook was clear.
Picking the catfish up, cradled
slick against my arms, I placed
it in the shallow water where, listing
on its side, we thought it dead;
until it wildly thrashed with life
as we yelled it back into the river.

The Burning Horses of Uncle Jack's Eyes

I saw my apartment building
at Charles and Commercial Drive
ablaze in torrents of red and blue flames.
They shimmered like sunlight
on the surface of uncle Jack's pond
in Pennsylvania where I fished
for catfish on July afternoons,
as uncle Jack masturbated in his farmhouse
bedroom while reciting The Song of Solomon
and mistaking my small shape for a fish.

Through each flaming window
the head of a wild horse stares. Its eyes
are Uncle Jack's eyes if he were a minnow
or a small animal, but he is neither.
He is a murdered horse with a killer's soul.
The living and dead are gathering
outside the building. My great-grandmother
has come. Her hands are filled with coal
and her face is blackened with coal dust.
She offers coal to the living and dead
but no one will take it. She drops to her knees
and begins to eat coal.

The heads of horses in the windows
are the laughing mouth of uncle Jack
as he drinks whisky and watches
the nightly news, sweat pouring
down his face like tributaries
of the river Jordan into his uneaten TV dinner.
My dead cousin Elijah has journeyed
to witness the burning horses of uncle Jack's eyes

on the back of a giant, flying crayfish. Its pincers
are the size of 1980s economy cars. We trapped
crayfish in jars to watch them fight
as sunlight crept up our bare backs
like uncle Jack's fingers. My born-again Christian
neighbour, Richard, who hid from the Vietnam War
in a beard white as a seder tablecloth,
has returned from the land of the dead
as a man-shaped whirlwind of ashes.
He's reciting a fake Kaddish
for his own death from fragments
of biblical tracts and excerpts
of speeches by Ronald Reagan.
The burning horses of uncle Jack's eyes
weep quietly as the living and dead
stone them with rocks the size of perfect baseballs.
I'm crouched in a closet. Uncle Jack's fists fall
on my head like hail stones that destroyed
the crops of Egypt. The dead and living
begin to sing as stones shatter windows
and the horses struggle to climb out,
front legs kicking wildly,
chests slick with bloody foam.

I'm twelve years old running
from the farmhouse through night,
grass wet beneath my feet
as the dead circle uncle Jack's pond
chanting a eulogy for a horse
he murdered at the age of twelve.
I hear arms of the kitchen clock
clacking like bones of Solomon
and his lovers, forty-one dream years
later, as I arrive at Charles and Commercial Drive
as windows explode like uncle Jack's eyes

ashes descending like flakes
of black snow into my great-grandmother's
uplifted and coal-stained hands.

That Day in America

I snuck down the basement stairs
to hide what I'd stolen. I'm not going
to tell you what it was because
it doesn't matter. I will tell you
on that day in America that upstairs
in our apartment my mother offered
her sons into the hands of a god
whose face mutated from bad lieutenant
to carnival huckster with a hard-on
in his polyester pants. That might
sound cruel but my mother was a labyrinth
of mirrors and rattlesnakes and took
what comfort she could find.
I will tell you on that day in America
that the skies over Harmarville
were a cold, hard blue like the robin's
eggs we'd later find by the power plant
and crush beneath our heels,
and small patches of filthy snow
in ditches and empty lots clung
to earth as spring came on. I will
tell you on that day in America Reagan
was hit by a bullet that ricocheted
off a black limo to lodge in his lungs
an inch from his heart and press secretary
James Brady was shot in the head.
I will tell you on that day in America
my mother sobbed as she told us
how she watched JFK's
brains get blown out in Dallas on TV
when she was fifteen. How she
grieved as if he were a close friend

or had done her a great personal kindness.
I will tell you on that day in America
I didn't care about JFK or Reagan,
as I hid in the basement storage locker
getting high. I saw John F. Hinckley
writing a love letter to Jodie Foster
and knew his eyes were the same colour
as my own.

Serpent and I

In Beaufort, South Carolina
on the dirt road near the trailer
a rattlesnake unravelled
its long muscle, slid in dust
between my small, bare legs
and torn sneakers untouched
by the spade-shaped head
as urine ran down my thighs.
I stood rigid, eyes
clamped against the sun,
mossy trees and the road,
until mother found and brought
me inside and made me sleep.
A dream of the rattler
coiling up my leg, its scaly grip.
climbing our bodies entwined
to fly through night
at white-hot stars.
The trailer, dirt road,
the earth itself,
a skein of dead skin
falling away
as serpent and I lifted
towards starry Eden.

Coward

I haven't talked to my mother
in years. The last time I heard her voice
was on my voicemail. She said
a real man would call his mother,
but I was a coward and always
had been. Her first two husbands
were Vietnam vets. The second, Chuck,
beat her on weekends when he'd
get drunk watching war movies.
They lived in a duplex in Beaufort,
South Carolina. Their neighbours cranked
music whenever she and Chuck
fought, usually well after midnight.
Once Chuck in his underwear
chased her into the street
waving a rifle as she screamed
he was a coward and that my father,
a Marine, was a real man.
Chuck pointed the rifle at her
then lowered it, went inside
and broke my brother's arm.

Mr. Gustafson

We shouted *Gussie* and blew
kisses at him as we entered
the classroom. We threw wet wads
of toilet paper that stuck to the blackboard
when he turned his back to us.
We dragged our desks together
during tests to cheat, blocking him
with our elbows and laughing
as he tried to stop us. Sometimes
a girl, when called on to answer
a question, shouted *Fuck you Gussie!*
and we'd howl and stamp our approval.
He was a small man with a bald head
and spindly arms who wore grey suits.
J. Alfred Prufrock come to teach
literature to working-class teenagers
of Harmarville and Harwick;
whose authors were the smokestack
over the power plant, the poisoned river
carrying barges heaped with coal
ripped from the green hills,
taverns where our fathers drank,
and stark churches
where our mothers prayed
and the dark mines and mills
he was meant to send us to.

Why I'm Not a Nature Poet

I've spent most of my life in cities,
though I did live in small towns
and the bush as a child.
I'm not knowledgeable about the names
of birds and flowers or the habits of animals.
I've never grown anything but I did shoot
a deer in Pennsylvania.
A lucky shot with a shotgun slug
that stopped its heart. We tied it to
the top of the car and parked
outside a diner to a gaggle of men
who admired our kill and slipped us
cans of Iron City Brew. For boys were
expected to hunt, fish, and to go
on camping trips with fathers
if you had one or whoever might
take you if you didn't. Our odd rites
of manhood. But these were short outings
into woods or country, two or three days
at most. At sixteen I spent the night beneath
a picnic table at Deer Lake Park
passed out and woke up hungover
to find I'd missed the opening hours
of trout season. My friends all gone
downstream and my fishing gear
tossed about on the wet grass. I drank
the remains of bottles I could find
and slept the rest of the day
in the backseat of a stranger's car.

The Buck

A morning in late December
a fourteen-year-old boy sits in a tree.
A twelve-gauge shotgun
lies across his knees loaded with a lead slug.
It's the first time he's hunted alone
without his grandfather or an uncle
to pass on their knowledge.
He has sat in the stand since dawn.
Three hours. He will remain
two more then walk home through town
with the shotgun resting on his shoulder.
Maybe it's his being alone in the woods
or the white veil of new snow covering
everything, but the silence he thinks
is not an absence of sound but a living
presence both outside and in.
A strange thought for a boy as a buck
steps from the trees into the clearing.
Each antler tip a point of light,
a bone crown of constellated stars.
The buck's black eyes,
a dark forest that enters him,
he sees himself in the tree
through the eyes of the buck
and does not lift his gun. Later
that day as he walks home
through town from the hunt
old men who seldom speak
to him will ask, *See anything?*

Ghosts

There were ghosts in that shit hotel
living in the walls like rats. I could hear
them at night whispering to themselves.
I saw one. An old woman with a face
like January rain sitting in the stained
bathtub gnawing at her wrists,
her body twisted and fibrous like roots
rotting underground. When she saw me
her eyes unravelled a spool of black
and white film. Images flickered
through the room, a storm of birds.
I shouted *Stop!* and everything
went static, a dead channel
on a television set. I woke up
choking on vomit.
Light on in the bathroom
and the window was open. Someone
was laughing in another room.
I thought I was in hell.
I didn't know anything.

Language

When she pulls off her T-shirt
a black skull with crossbones
and burning eyes stares at me
from between her breasts.
It's nineteen eighty-four. I'm seventeen.
I've never seen a woman with tattoos
beyond a small smudge of a bird
above an ankle. I've never been taken
home by one either. She finishes disrobing
and walks naked around the room
to light candles. She pours two glasses
of red wine, hands me one
and sits on a leather love seat
with her legs spread. A black and white
Death's-head moth floats just above
her vagina. She sees me looking, laughs
and says *As above, so below.*
I'm silent and look away.
Take off your clothes.
Red eyes of the black skull
glare and the moth flutters
in twitching candlelight
as I undress. Shadows
open like a dark mouth
and I begin to learn a language
older than men.

Soul Mates

She talked about spirits
like a shooting gallery.
She said our souls were
a target the blind man
never missed no matter
how high we got.
She was full of shit like me,
but her eyes were lightning
in which I saw myself
and her naked in the rain
clutching baggies of meth
like talismans, waving
toy swords against
darkening clouds.
Yeah, we were a special kind
of fucked up but she made sense
to me. Like a child sent out
into the world with nothing
but a feral heart, wilder and stronger
than all the common sense
that looked the other way.

Strippers

A strip joint along Interstate 19
in Clearwater, Florida. A cinderblock
building painted black. A sign
on the roof flashing STRIPPERS
in red lights. It didn't have a name.
It was more like a bunker or a garage
than a bar. Inside was so dark
you could barely see strippers
or patrons. That wasn't an accident.
No one in that place looked good.
I'd buy meth from the doorman
and snort it in the washroom stall.
Then sit by the stage to nurse a drink,
chew the insides of my mouth
until they bled. The strippers were young women
with bony hips and sallow faces,
bikinis sagging off their bodies
like ubiquitous American flags
drooping from homes
I'd walk past on my way to and from the bar.
The girls worked for tips and drinks.
They'd lean in close, talk dirty
or offer to hook up with you
in your car for the right price.
For a year I went every evening after work
and stayed until they closed.
I only spoke to order drinks
or buy drugs. The dancers ignored
me except for a girl named Keisha.
She'd sit down a few times a night
to hand me a napkin. *Honey clean
yourself up, your mouth is bleeding.*

I'd wipe my lips and toss the napkin
to the floor. Keisha would stand,
shake her head and say,
What girl is ever gonna kiss
a mouth like that?

Salt

The Archangel Raphael cured a man's
blindness with fish guts. I'm learning to

disguise myself in metaphors. Apparently,
I'm not fooling anyone except myself.

I say the word "apparently" a lot
and also "a lot". An angel turned Lot's

wife into a pillar of salt for sneaking
a peek. Apparently, angels are

morally neutral. They just follow orders.
When I was thirteen I saw a woman

undressing through a window. Ten years
later I frequented strip joints

like an actor who can't remember
his lines. Whenever I tried to tip

the dancers, my pockets
overflowed with salt.

Beaufort, South Carolina

It was a southern moon. Big and gold.
Dangling in the night like an ancient coin.
She said we could pluck it from the sky,
spend it any way we wanted
and the next night there'd be another
just the same. It's easy to talk
like that when you're eighteen and beautiful.
I was young too but I knew better.
She was a Carolina girl with no end
to daddy's love or money.
I was trailer trash she'd taken in
for a couple nights on summer vacation.
She grabbed my hand and pulled me
down the beach saying the whole thing
was ours. Maybe it was. As we
fucked standing against the lifeguard station
she put her hand on my chest. Said she'd
never felt a heart beat that fast
and I should take it easy. The night
and everything she offered
as golden as that southern moon,
but I had to spend it all before morning.

Gimpy

I washed dishes in a club in Jacksonville,
Florida. I threw a dishrag into a toilet
in the men's room and called it
an offering to Poseidon. That was
my idea of poetry then. Where have all
the ginger worshippers of cracker
Jesus gone? Are they picking badly tuned
banjos in hell? Or maybe they're hiding
out in a timeshare in the Yucatan
living off street tacos and mailing postcards
to their spiritual leader, sociopath David Duke.
I bought an old terrier mutt with three legs
and one eye from a Russian on the beach
in Clearwater. He solicited customers
for fishing charters by reading their palms
to predict their impending catch
of record-breaking marlins. His hair
was greasier than the french fries
sold from the food trucks by the pier.
I named the dog Gimpy. He got run
over by a US Postal truck the day
before Christmas in the parking lot
of a strip joint. The door girl held
his limp body in her lap and cried.
She told me his droopy little ears
looked like tattered bandages.
When I told her his name she told me
I was an asshole. I had an 8-ball, two ounces
of weed and a handgun in a gym bag
I'd taken from a car my recently
dishonourably discharged alcoholic cousin
had hot-wired outside Applebees that morning.

I asked her if she wanted to party. As she
lifted her head to look at me I saw
what her eyes saw and started running
along Interstate 19 and slipped
into an Olive Garden. I pushed through
a gaggle of parents and girl scouts
in the lobby and locked myself
in a bathroom stall and snorted coke
until the manager knocked on the door
and said this was a family restaurant
and he had called the cops. I flushed
the coke and quietly slipped the gun
into the toilet tank. It hit bottom
with a dull thud. Like the sound
the postal truck made when it
backed over Gimpy.

That Fly Lays Eggs

There is a comet at the outer edges
of the solar system that takes 250,000

years to orbit the sun. The grey ghost
of T.S. Eliot was sighted thirty miles

outside of Wichita reading *The Waste Land*
to a scarecrow, as stars ricocheted

across the sky like billiard balls
or bleached bones of dead men.

I try to read the past but it evades me
like a Tarot card reader with news

of an impending death. A fly is trapped
in my lungs, struggling to escape.

When I cough I see torn bits
of tiny, transparent wings. I hate

sentimentality, but it hates me too.
That fly lays eggs like I write poems.

Strange Bird

When she stopped caring
he caught the bus to the next

state. He'd been through
this before. He'd find a bar,

a woman, a place.
A strange bird rode

the long trip in his jacket
pocket. It had one eye,

moulting feathers.
Sometimes he'd stroke

the small head
with his index finger

and the bird would sing.
Its song was not beautiful.

Love

I was naked on the concrete floor of the basement.
I was crying and jerking off at the same time.
I'd torn the phone out of the wall and knocked
over the bottle of gin and the bottle of sleeping pills,
two or three pills left glistening in a small pool
of booze. I couldn't tell the difference between a sex act
and killing myself. *It's not a fucking surprise
is it you little cocksucker?* Don't worry, I'm talking
to myself not you. The girl had called to tell me
she'd cheated on me again and because I was drunk
and full of self-loathing and had eaten most of the pills
I let her tell me how she'd fucked him while I fucked
my hand. After I'd listened long enough, after the hatred
we felt for each other and ourselves was too much,
I ripped the phone from the wall and tried to finish
myself off and failed both ways. I woke up two days
later on the concrete floor, my head raw with pain
that shot through my brain when I moved my eyes.
I tried to stand and saw my body was covered in dried vomit,
as if I'd rolled around in it like a pig in his own shit.
Do you feel ashamed of me, do you feel disgusted
and maybe turned on in a way that makes you
want to retch? That's how I've felt since I was a kid.
I thought it was love.

There Is Something in the Tree

Bring it down.
I'm sick of listening to it.
It pretends to be a bird,
but it has a square black head
with steel mandibles
and two artificial legs
the colour of money.

It doesn't sing. It talks
like a high school guidance
counsellor with a stroking hand
in his pocket. He's all sweaty
decorum and a wisdom
dull as an old box
of *Reader's Digests*.

There is something in the tree.
Bring it down.
I'm sick of it watching me.
Eyes flat as felt markers.
The face of something dead
but historical and important
like the Lincoln Memorial
or the Roman Coliseum.

There is something in the tree.
Bring it down.
At night I hear it rubbing
its steel mandibles together,
a sound of sharpening knives,
a grating of stones
as ocean is sucked
out before the wave
that smashes everything.

Perfect

His face was bleached legal paper.
A blankness that concealed his thoughts.

My heart explodes on a daily basis.
I collect singed feathers and wear

them in my hair. I'm a prehistoric bird.
When I was twelve God was a fat man

with bad dandruff and quick fists. My counsellor
said my imagination had a bad attitude.

An asteroid shower is the universe
saying hello. Only assholes and conmen

say shit like that. An empire of pain
is a sum zero game. Someday

I'm going to stop feeling.
I'll be perfect.

Poetry Is Everywhere

There are twelve ways to ride
a tornado. I prefer nitroglycerin

and a pair of dice. Kurt Cobain's
lyrics were radioactive fireflies

dive-bombing an industrial park
on summer nights. History is a bank

guarded by teachers. If you're sick
of listening to me, imagine how I feel.

Talking to my ancestors is a feedback
loop. Like a brick through the kitchen

window, spraying glass,
silver trout leaping in your eyes.

Almost Summer

I smoked meth for two days
in a basement suite. Kept hearing
the pastor's voice in his airless office,
seeing his sweaty face
and the hair on the back of his hands,
put my fist through the window.
My knuckles opened and blood
flowed down my hands and arms,
tore the doors off cupboards
in the kitchen and smashed
the mirror in the bathroom,
took a chair and drove four legs
into the plaster wall, threw
beer bottles across the room
to smash into pieces, punched
holes through plaster. Blood
was on everything. The landlord
came from upstairs and banged
on the locked door. I flung it open
and tackled him against the concrete steps.
Most nights it was him who made the noise
screaming at his silent wife. His sons
pulled me off and chased me
into the bedroom. I slammed the door
and locked it, pushed the dresser
against it. When I was halfway out
the window the police grabbed me
and threw me on the front lawn
twisting my arms behind my back,
cuffed my hands. It was dawn
and the damp grass was cool
against my face. Birds sang

from green hedges as big trucks
rumbled Clark Drive. A cop said
Calm down son,
I don't want to hurt you.
I tasted dirt in my mouth.
It was almost summer.

II

A Girl from Kansas City

I met her in the poetry section
of a downtown bookstore.
She was looking for *The Drunken Boat*
by Rimbaud. She said she wanted something
she could relate to. *Oh, so you're into boats?*
I asked. *No,* she said and laughed.
I offered to buy her a drink
so we went to a bar off Granville Street.
One of those fabricated British pubs.
She had one blue eye and one green eye,
her hair was straw-coloured.
She was from Kansas City
but spoke with a fake Irish accent.
When I asked why she answered,
Why not? As she talked her fingers
danced across the table
like it was a piano and each word
was a note she played. She said
I was a sensitive tough guy
more sensitive than tough
probably not tough at all
but that was good.
She hated tough guys
said they were stunted,
self-centred, abusive pricks.
I asked her name but she
said she wasn't into names.
When I ran out of money
she bought the drinks until closing.
As the lights came up her face
was flushed and the green eye
seemed larger and brighter

than the blue one and the light
seemed to catch her straw-coloured hair
like a pale crown of fire. She stared
at a spot past me and began to recite
the opening lines of Keats'
Ode to a Nightingale and got
as far as "dull opiate" and stopped.
I'm flying to Ohio tomorrow, she said.
*I've been here two days and I already
hate you and this fucking town.*

Shooting Stars

Every time she went into a liquor store
she came out with two or three mickeys
under her jacket. We'd go to my basement
suite to drink them. We'd sit at a table
by the furnace in semi-darkness
with one lit candle. She said she didn't
like to see well-lit faces when she
drank. I didn't take it personally.
I needed to get drunk and she brought
the booze. We didn't talk much. I'd watch
the candlelight flicker against her face
and the way she shut her eyes
when the bottle touched her lips.
It made me think of people
taking communion or making wishes
on a meteor as it flamed out through
the atmosphere. I guess we were both
looking for some kind of salvation
and falling at the same time. I wondered
if there would be much of us left
when we hit bottom.

Six Bottles of Wine

I haven't washed the dishes for over a week.
The sink and counter a precarious pile
of dirty pots, plates, bowls and glasses.
The whole mess on the verge of slippage,
of shattering into mundane but dangerous pieces.
I haven't bathed in five days or brushed
my teeth. I can barely stand the sight or smell
of myself. I am a riot of self-pity in a filthy apartment.
And yes, yes, I've been drinking. I'm gloriously,
hideously drunk. I've been reading poetry
out loud, shouting through walls
at my neighbours. Every night the landlord pounds
on my door, tells me to shut up. I will
have to pay for my behaviours with sickness,
debt and shame. But I have six bottles of wine
before I have to remember that she is dead.

The Prophet

He was lying on the couch smoking
when I got back from the liquor store.
He said he got in through the window
and I should be more careful. But I
had nothing of value unless someone
wanted a black and white TV
I used pliers to change channels
with or a coffee can filled with butts
of stale tobacco I rolled into homemade
smokes, or a plastic table stolen from a backyard
down the block. He sat up when I
gave him a beer and thanked me.
I leaned against the opposite wall.
The last time I'd seen him I'd helped
trash his place during a wake for a friend.
He chased me down Hastings Street
waving a butcher's knife screaming
You're dead, motherfucker! But he
moved to Toronto. It had been three years.
Now his body was all sharp bones
and huge eyes watching from a face
so severe he looked like an Old Testament
prophet wandering sun-stricken deserts
with visions of fire and blood.
AIDS he said. *Shared needles.*

We drank through the afternoon
and into the night. We didn't
say much, we'd never been close,
gaps in our conversation
growing longer as shadows
filled the living room. I had no idea

why he'd come to me. When I heard
him crying in the darkness
I coughed nervously. He stopped
and apologized, his voice
as empty as my home, my life.

The Sick Buffalo

At night I hear a sick buffalo
moaning from my neighbour's apartment.
How the hell did he get it in there?
Where does it shit? Its moans
are the sounds of subway trains
disappearing into dark tunnels.
Its mangy pelt exudes a rankness
that burns through our walls,
a mixture of ammonia and death.
First time I smelled it
I was sick for days. I avoid my neighbour
because his reeking clothes
make me gag. How does he stand it?
I hear him talking to the beast.
He asks why its eyes are emptier
than a bombed-out village,
sadder than a refugee camp.
In southern Alberta a German tourist
went into a field to photograph a herd
and was trampled while his family
watched from the rental car.
This buffalo could be dangerous.
I wonder if it was involved.
Do its horns shine like crescent moons
in the darkness of the bathroom
or are they dull and yellow
like the teeth of an old dog?
The moans grow louder,
become a deep guttural song,
a droning, rhythmic hum,
the distant pounding
of thousands of hooves. Vibrations

grow stronger until the building begins to shake. The buffalo isn't sick, it's dreaming.

I Don't Date Drunks

No higher powers in here she scoffed,
more like a flea market for unwanted souls.
She slow-motion zigzagged across the room
to half sit, half collapse into the chair
beside me. *I wonder if a soul can be the colour
of dog shit, because that's what mine feels
like,* she joked. Then she swayed into my shoulder
placing her hand on my thigh to stop herself
from falling into my lap. I'd never felt a hand
or body so light, almost weightless as feathers
or paper. Her breath and skin
had the sweet and sour reek of alcohol
so I stiffened and pulled away.
Don't worry fucker! she said as her eyes
swam across her face to find mine.
I don't date drunks.

My Self-Pity Is Bigger than Yours

I tried to watch *Waiting for Guffman* last night,
but I got so paranoid I turned it off. My life is sadder

than a country song without a good chorus
or royalties. I broke the blinds

had to staple a sheet over the window. So now
I sleep against the bare mattress. What kind of man

owns one sheet and can't stop drinking? Easy:
an alcoholic. My therapist says given my childhood

I'm lucky to be alive. Maybe next life let's set
the bar a little higher. Oh someday poetry

is gonna explode out of me like a truck
full of fireworks on the darkest night

of the year. With my luck the truck
will be parked on the lowest level

of an underground parkade. If self-pity
and grandiosity were talents

Rodney DeCroo would be a household
name. I'd only drink the finest Irish whisky,

never leave my apartment
and buy a set of designer sheets.

Always True

You hated pity and you hated goodbyes.
Some weekends you crawled on hands
and knees in your apartment because
of back pain. But Monday morning
you climbed in your truck
and drove to the construction site. A small,
muscular man with thick white hair
blue eyes that could go cold
as glacial water or bright as summer skies.
You told me many times how you
nearly drank yourself to death
in a house filled with illegal guns
you sold to criminals until you
were arrested. You said it
was the best thing that ever happened
to you; the cops kicking in the door
to find you passed out at the kitchen table
with a cigarette burning a black mark
into the tabletop and a loaded gun
in your left hand. A year later you
walked into a courtroom without a lawyer
and a crowd of sober drunks in the gallery
to plead guilty. You had a dream
the night before that the judge
became an enormous eagle
and flew you through miles of sky
to a beautiful small town where people
sat in church basements smoking
and drinking coffee as they told
miraculous stories
that were always true.

The Podium

I store a podium in my apartment
for a group that meets weekly
in the community centre
across the street. I can't tell you
who I see there or what is said.
Like a butler in a British murder
mystery, I remain silent. It looks
heavy but it's light enough
to carry on my own. Probably
weighs no more than twenty lbs.
It's strange having this object
in my home. It's like a pulpit
or a confessional standing
next to the big screen TV
while I watch crime thrillers
on Netflix or internet porn
which I use as a substitute
for intimacy—okay, that's enough.
I'm going to hang a sheet
over the podium. A person
can only handle a certain
amount of honesty
and self-reflection. I'll wait
until next week when I haul
it across the street to meet
with my friends who listen
a hell of a lot better than I do.

Steve Dabrowski

I Google search Steve Dabrowski
and find his father's recent obituary.
I read about Steve as the son
who preceded his father in death
at the age of twenty-two. I do another search
find four separate arrest records
that he was a mechanic
who lived his entire short life
in the hometown I escaped at sixteen.
I didn't know his father
was a member of the Harwick Polish Club;
a retired landscaper who liked crossword puzzles
and watching television. I also didn't know
why Steve slammed a studded wrist band
into the back of my head, threatened me
outside a party with a knife
or sucker-punched me in the face
after history class. I didn't know why we
fought several times after football practices.
I didn't know that I'd hated a dead boy
for thirty years who I had never known.

Your Eyes

A row of plastic bags rinsed in kerosene
flutter on a clothesline like asthmatic lungs.

The sun isn't a canker sore; the problem
is the mind. A burnt match or the bones

of a dead finger aren't nearly as cold
as the eyes of a bureaucrat. Like Lazarus

I have bad breath and hate locked doors.
I tried to stop a war by becoming an alcoholic

found peace in a detox facility.
Federico Garcia Lorca was cut down

by the sky and the guns of Spanish fascists.
What's in a name? Not much. That's why

the best poets are painters. Your eyes
are the paint they see through.

The Bar

I told him several times the drink
was going to kill him. So did his family
doctor, the surgeon and several nurses
too. But every time he'd laugh and say
that life was killing him and booze
was his medicine. Once I suggested AA
and he said his higher power
was Jack Daniels. When I pushed him
out of the hospital in a wheelchair
he wanted to go to his favourite bar. We argued
until I put him in a cab and told him
he could do whatever he wanted
but I wasn't going to watch him
drink himself to death. When his ex-wife
called two days later to say they'd
found him in his room I thanked her
and threw my phone against the wall.
A gesture he would've scornfully
called melodramatic. I can see
the profile of his face as the taxi
pulled away. His destination
wasn't the bar and he knew it
better than any of us.

What the Dead Hear

I often talk to the dead at night. My cat gives
me a dirty look that says this place is lousy
with ghosts, can't you invite a living person
over sometime. But what she doesn't know
is that the dead let you talk for hours
and never interrupt. They've got nothing
but time. Though I'm starting to suspect
they don't understand what I'm telling them.
It's like lying in bed at 2:00 AM listening
to the rain falling against the windows and roof.
That's what my words sounds like to them.
Except they're outside in the dark,
looking in.

Booms and Busts

As I walk along the Bow River
I think of the young genius
John Keats. He wrote five
of the greatest odes in the English
language before dying alone in Italy
from tuberculosis, his love estranged
and his poetry mocked. I walk past
couples taking evening strolls
in the mild, spring air. Their hushed
voices making a light music against
the backdrop of the river's
crash and hum. It'll be dark
soon but not before they return
to their cars for the drive
back to the comforts
of the sprawling suburbs.
I've come to Calgary
a city of booms and busts,
to play my songs tonight
in a noisy bar. Later
as the muted TV's images
flicker in the motel's darkness
I'll doubt the worth
              of those songs—
and there will be
no answer.

Postcards

I could smell smoke from three miles
away. In the country you walk until you

get there. Seeing an entire field
burning at night is a glimpse of eternity.

But don't kid yourself, the bars
are securely fastened. Even such visitations

are merely postcards dropped in our laps
the way I toss scraps to the dog

while he scratches his ass. My cousin
talks about God the way people

talk about football games. I figure if you
can say it there's not much to talk about.

It shouldn't hurt so much, these stadiums
of emptiness, but it does. Just like God

waiting in the executive suite
for someone every ten thousand years

to slip a postcard
under the door.

Reading Frost

The cat watches from the couch
as I read aloud "Design" by Frost.
When I finish he shuts his eyes
sets his head upon his paws.
The refrigerator gurgles then chugs
along for a minute or so then stops.
The heater clicks and the walls creak
as the building shifts its old bones
in the wind. I hear my neighbour's
muffled voice downstairs speaking
to someone who never replies.
My eyes drift to the darkness outside
my warm, well-lit den
and I read the poem again.

The Building Talks to Me

This building makes noises I don't
understand. I can't pierce the meaning

of its guttural speech. My friends
are startled by the sounds in the walls,

but I smile and say
It's just the pipes. They're old.

How am I supposed to understand
the language of wood, nails, pipes

and plaster when I barely comprehend
the human speech that swirls

around me? My own thoughts
loss leaders meant to distract

me from my own painful truths.
The truth is, even if I understood

what this old building is saying
I wouldn't trust a word of it.

A Political Poem

My friends tell me my poems
should be more politically conscious;
an artist should be an activist
strive to change the world
through their art. My mind
immediately goes to Shelley's
famous line about poets
and legislators but I'm not
going to beat myself up
with that stick. Besides Shelley
was a rich bastard who slummed
it with the bohemians after he got
kicked out of Oxford for writing
a pamphlet about atheism. If I'd
been alive then the closest
I would've got to Oxford
would've been a broom
and a dustpan sweeping
up Shelley's famous pamphlet.
Okay, so now you're saying I got a chip
on my shoulder. Well, you're wrong.
It's more like a fucking brick—
and one of these days
I'm gonna throw it through
the front window of a bank.
Afterwards, I'll buy everyone
drinks at the local tavern
while I read them
my new poem
about the redistribution
of wealth.

Frozen Cherries

I've been eating frozen cherries
at night while watching movies.
I get them from the Super-Valu
down the street from my place.
When they're on sale I buy enough
to load my freezer until there's no room
for anything else. Did I mention I'm obsessive
have the mind of an addict
even when it comes to frozen fruit?
Before cherries it was apple fritters
and long before that it was alcohol,
cocaine or codeine. But I've recovered
from the nastier addictions with the help
of many friends and a therapist.
But sometimes I'm bothered by questions.
Like where do they grow the cherries?
Who harvests them, what were the working
conditions like and what were they paid?
But it doesn't pay to think
about these things for everything
in my apartment raises similar questions.
Tonight, I just want to watch a movie and let
the frozen flesh melt in my mouth
until it's tender and sweet,
but even a cherry is never
just a cherry is it?

Warmed in the Vacuum of Space

I received my weekly, digital Walmart
flyer today. From dining to unwinding

they have the perfect patio furniture
collection for everyone at prices

cheaper than pig shit. I'm crude like oil
but it pays the bills. If Sam Walton

saw an "infinitely gentle / Infinitely
suffering thing" he'd club it to death

like a baby seal then make a donation
to the arts. Never forget that TS Eliot

was a banker even on his best days. I listen
to Beethoven's "Ode to Joy" like a near-death

experience. He wasn't a composer.
He was an alchemist. That's why he

went deaf. So he could hear the music.
I want to be a comet's tail warmed

in the vacuum of space
when passing near the sun.

Tying the Centuries Together Like a Funeral Wreath

I want a song like a busted hand or a smashed clock.
I want a poem like a bruised eye swollen shut
after a fight. I want to fuck like river rats in the sludge
of the Ohio River on the hard edges of Pittsburgh
where desire is desperate, bred of lightning and fear
and drowning is always possible. I want a moon
that's an empty ball of craters, the gaunt face
of a scream echoing through nightmares the day
does its best to deny. I want a melody with all the wonder
of a collapsing star and the taste of Mary Katherine Murphy's
lips behind the power plant where rusted barges
huddled in the river's night like ancient warships
full of mythic heroes instead of mounds of coal.
I want to sit in a theatre where the bones of my dead
rattle in the throats of actors like a just discovered prayer,
tying the centuries together like a funeral wreath
or a braid of my grandmother Matilda Ferguson's
girlish hair reaching from Glasgow to Ellis Island
to Buttermilk Falls, Pennsylvania to Vancouver,
British Columbia. I want a eulogy that says it
stopped with me, this line of broken labourers,
shattered soldiers, depressed housewives,
schizophrenics, suicides, alcoholics, criminals,
religious fanatics, the casualties of war and capital,
this long march of not so quiet desperation
laid to rest in the Pacific, where my ashes
will be dumped like the charcoal smear
of a dirty fingerprint and then nothing
but water and sky.

III

Human Traces

Strings of white lights hanging
from your back porch are a tiny galaxy.
What if stars descended to live with us?
Our flesh would melt instantly, our bones
burnt beyond ashes, all human traces obliterated.
But maybe there are dead stars that might walk
among us. Dim faces signalling a memory
beyond time—a brightness fiercer than all
world-killing bombs combined.

The Caterpillar

I stitched the cut with black thread
a needle from the sewing kit
you left under the bathroom sink.
The needle was rusty. I used it anyway.
It pierced my skin roughly, tugged
at the edges of the wound. The row
of bunched black stitches a caterpillar
sleeping on my arm. I pricked it
with your abandoned sliver
of corroded steel. It woke, slowly
unfurled wings, and took flight.

I Knew a Songwriter

who was well-behaved
and his songs were also well-behaved.
But he talked about it all the time:
how Johnny Cash took pills,
Hank Williams overdosed, Janis Joplin
drank herself to death, Billie Holiday
was a junkie, Steve Earle went to prison,
how fucked up they were,
but oh man,
they wrote such great songs.

As he talked I could hear
his teeth and jaws working

as he chewed their brains and hearts
to cannibalize what it was

in them that wrote those songs
he could never write.

You Wanted to Be

a stand-up comedian but you
weren't funny. Your jokes
went over like farts at a dinner party.
Once you said my poems
were like chickens, incapable of flight.
Okay, that was good. I always
brought out the best in you.

The Luthier

I met a lawyer at a folk conference
who collects expensive guitars
stores them in a sealed room
at a perfect temperature. He says
I've badly mistreated my only guitar.
And he's right; the fretboard is eroded,
the tuning pegs need replacing,
the body is scarred, discoloured and cracked.
My guitar and I have played
hundreds of shows in nearly as many bars,
travelled thousands of miles in automobiles,
trains and planes. Nearly no one has played
my guitar but me. Together we've written
nearly all my songs. After a show a month
ago a man from South Carolina came to the stage
to talk with me. He was thin and stooped,
eyes like black walnut. He said he was a luthier.
He'd built and repaired guitars for forty-seven years.
He asked if he could hold mine. I passed it to him.
He sat down on a chair and cradled it
for several minutes, head bowed as if to catch a
secret, or a few whispered last words. I watched him
impatiently. I wanted to get paid and go home
as drunk patrons shouted and stumbled around us.
Finally, he stood up and held out the guitar.
I took it, he gave a stiff, little bow and I felt
the vibrations through the scarred wood—
the song still beating in our hands.

Poor Man's Doves

At night pigeons roost on the window
sill outside my bathroom. As I brush
my teeth I make out their shapes
like small, round loaves of bread
through frosted glass. Some people
call them rats with wings, but I think
of them as the poor man's dove.
They make soft, guttural sounds
half song, half complaint.
They're indifferent to my presence,
don't seem to mind the running tap,
the flushed toilet or the flicked-on light.
This afternoon I opened the window
while they were away. The sill
was caked with shit and feathers.
I boiled water and poured it
on their roost until it was clean.
I did it more for me than them.
They don't mind their mess.
But I hope when they return
this evening and find the clean,
white ledge they remember
it as home.

I Met Death in the Cereal Aisle

at Super-Valu shortly after midnight.
He wore a black dress that hung off his
scrawny frame down to his dirty sneakers.
He looked like Prince Charles
if he'd grown up poor and white
in Kentucky with an opiate addiction.
His ears reminded me of bat wings.
Despite his slovenly appearance his nails
were immaculately manicured. They shined
beneath harsh fluorescent lights
like small, perfect moons. As he reached
past me for a box of Captain Crunch
he excused himself politely. His voice
was burnt macaroni stuck to the bottom
of an old pot. But he smelled
like birthday cake. A vanilla scent
some girls wore at community college
when I was young and undefeated.

A Confessional Poem

I'm always on my laptop
circling the same websites
like an irritable cloud of seagulls
squawking over a garbage dump.
I get constant throat infections
because I inhale Flovent twice daily
to prevent asthma but I don't gargle
with saltwater afterwards. I use internet porn
because my last two relationships
ended with me in the psych ward.
I think a lot about killing myself
but it's mostly suicidal ideation
so I don't think it's serious;
like the weather, it's always been there.
I have C-PTSD but I go to therapy.
I'm supposedly getting better. I've stopped
arguing with strangers at Tim Hortons
and getting in fist fights on public transit.
I don't get gigs at folk festivals
anymore because they can't handle
the truth or — GULP! — my music sucks,
or I'm just another asshole with a story
they've heard too many times.
That was a rhetorical question
so don't answer or I'll block you
on Facebook. I read through parts
of Marx's *Capital* every year.
I like the stuff about alienation.
I think I'd like to be a Marxist.
I think I have use-value
but my exchange-value is low,
almost non-existent these days.

Two days ago I put my cat down
because she had tumours
and I couldn't afford the surgery.
When her body went slack
in the vet's hands I wanted
to head-butt him, but it's not
his fault. It's just death—
a small, still body
that looks like my cat,
but isn't.

My Therapist Tells Me

I'm one of the most intelligent
individuals he's ever met despite
my lack of education. Either he
hasn't met many people
or he's trying to counter
the bad voices in my head
that tell me unceasingly
in myriad ways
I'm a stupid piece of shit.
It could be that one
of those voices
has taken over this poem
disguising its nastiness
as self-deprecation. So, this
business of voices
—as you might surmise—
is a tricky business. Who
can you trust if you
can't trust the voices
in your head or your own poem?
You might also say that this
isn't a poem. Where are the metaphors,
clever line breaks and images?
Or even rhymes if you're
into that sort of thing. And where's
the music? This all sounds
prosaic to me. Merely a bunch
of sentences going nowhere
like a gerbil on a wheel
beady black eyes staring
intensely ahead as feet
fly to the rapid-fire beat

of his heart. For he knows
if he can just run fast enough
he'll break this cage
and prove everybody wrong.

The Writers Festival

She asks me questions about line breaks
using technical terms I don't know.
When I reply I just do what feels right
she looks away as if I'd said something lewd,
clutches her wine glass to her chest,
joins a knot of guests discussing
found poetry as disruptive practice
undermining the fascistic implications
of the lyric poem. I make for the table
laid out with sushi, samosas, chicken wings,
sausage rolls, pastries, cheese, crackers,
wine and beer all paid for by Penguin Books.
As I covertly stuff samosas into the pockets
of my overcoat the artistic director
of the festival asks me if poets ever eat.
I'm the third he's caught filling
their pockets. I laugh but see he's
not joking and put the now lint speckled
samosas back on the tray. I look at the free booze
and start to feel a little thirsty. I think that prick's
lucky I'm not drinking or a couple stolen samosas
would be the least of his problems.

Moniack Mhor

I'm lying on a single bed
at Scotland's national writers' centre.
Winds bash the building
as sleet clinks against the glass.
I look out the window.
The view by day: moors,
Highland cows, the valley
speckled with farmhouses,
strips of roads,
sheep with their coats
of shaggy wool dotting green pastures,
and sloping brown mountains
are blotted out by blackness.
There's not a single star.
Sky one roiling black cloud.
All is wet, dark and wild.
Earlier today as I walked
through the forest I cut my legs
against the thistles. As I scratched
and bitched at dinner I was told
the thistle plant provides the antidote:
its leaves to rub against your skin
for relief and cure. I wondered if it
was a trick Highlanders play
on gullible tourists.
Or if the plant that hurts also heals.
On Saturday night we'll have haggis
and a poet will recite Robbie Burns.
When I fall to sleep I dream of St. Kilda
where gannets were hunted
 for their flesh and eggs. I'm hanging
from an island cliff as seabirds

scream into my face. As my fingers
lose their hold a man shouts
from a ragged shore. I think he wants
to help. But I don't know the language
and he doesn't live here anymore.

Learning to Ride

Lucy leads Chip through the parking lot
to the riding barn. Chip's head bobs low
as they slowly walk, reins trailing
from Lucy's hand. It's one of those
Vancouver days when it could rain
any second but doesn't. At the entrance
I open the gate so rider and horse
can pass into the spacious shadows
of the arena. When I follow, the instructor
holds up her hand. I'm told to stay outside
where it's safe. Lucy climbs the blocks
to mount her horse as the instructor
holds the reins. When I smile and wave
she looks away from me to Chip,
her face serious and focused
like when she's reading Harry Potter
or watching *Midsomer Murders*.
I think about when I was eleven,
the age she is now, how I hid by the river
drinking beer with my friends,
smoking cigarettes until I puked.
The instructor shouts my name
as Lucy and Chip trot away
from the blocks into the arena.
Yes? I ask. *Lucy is going to do
her first jump today,* she says.
You're supposed to watch.

Mistatim

Archer tells me on the phone
from Toronto that mistatim
is the Cree word for horse
and literally means "big dog".

We didn't speak for two years
because my father's war
came home to us
when I was a boy. It stalks

my mind with the presence
of faceless enemies
he carried home
in his words and fists—

farmers and villagers
fleeing the bullets
fired from his M-16.
Now years later

like my father, I see enemies
who are not enemies
and my finger curls
around the cold trigger.

I woke up to a horse
filling the darkness of my room.
The enormous body above me
like a god, like a memory

older than this city
where I live in my electric

cave. Its head bent over
my face, warm breath

from huge nostrils
touching my skin and hair.
In the morning I called
my friend Archer

and we began
to talk again
about horses,
wars and dreams.

Safeway

There are six of us waiting
outside the entrance to Safeway.
We follow social distancing
protocols, staying six feet apart,
wearing our masks.
We nod at each other
but don't engage. A teenager
is speaking what I think
is Cantonese into his phone.
I have no idea what he's
saying but it sounds
like he's reassuring someone.
After the call he shuts
his eyes for several seconds.
When he opens them he sees
me watching and turns away.
There are four cars in a parking
lot that holds a few hundred
and traffic on Broadway
is a mere trickle for rush hour.
It's quiet enough
I can hear the bright chatter
of sparrows in the trees
lining the sidewalk.
When the doors whoosh
open and two people push
by with loaded carts
I tell the next person
to go ahead of me.
I'm going to sit on the curb
and listen to the sparrows.

Isolation

I've been alone in my apartment
for nearly two weeks. I'm asthmatic
have had pneumonia
three times so my doctor wants
me to isolate since Covid-19
attacks the respiratory system.
My friends call every day
to see how I'm doing
leave groceries outside
my door. I want to say
these gifts arrive
like my poems do, seemingly
out of nowhere. But it's important
to be exact these days and I
remind myself that I'm fortunate
to have good friends.
I've started going for walks
late at night on residential streets
when few people are out. Cats appear
from the shadows of front gates
and hedges. I don't pet them
but stand still as they brush
themselves against my shins.
Last night I talked with a chubby Siamese
as he rubbed his head
against my sneakers. I told him
I'm reading Ovid's *Metamorphoses*
and the gods are total psychos
who rape and murder the Greeks
whenever they feel like it.
They're petty, vain, and often
inflict unjust and horrible
punishments transforming

people into beasts, trees and
stones. I tell him the world of
myths is a terrifying place
where certainties can evaporate
at the whim of an offended god,
you can be eaten alive by a Cyclops,
or beaten to death by drunk Centaurs
at your best friend's wedding.
As I told my Siamese friend
the details of a particularly grisly myth
all the street lights clicked off.
The cat swatted at my shoe
and ran beneath a parked car.
As my eyes adjusted to the darkness
and the dim light filtering
from the windows of houses
I stood and waited.
Anything could happen.
The lights could turn back on, I
might be turned into a tree
or murdered by a god.

Leftovers

I'll have them for days
and each day
they taste better. I'll cook
a beef stew,
a big pot of spaghetti or chili
and scarcely touch the food
until it has sat in the fridge
for at least a night.
Sometimes at restaurants
I'll order a second meal
to take home for later.
I've always loved such things
whether it's food well kept,
a second-hand jacket
worn comfortable
or an old guitar played
by other hands than mine.
I've always distrusted
the new and shiny thing. I prefer
seasoned stories that wait
for a patient tongue.

Poetry Class

Lucy explains foreshadowing
to me over Zoom as we read
a Robert Service poem and stop
after each stanza to discuss
what we've just read.
She says it's kind of like when you
know what's coming before it happens.
You mean in a story? I ask.
No, in real life!
*Oh, so sometimes you know
what's going to happen?*
Of course, she says, *don't you?*
I think how my dad
would joke about going
to the store for milk
and not coming back.
How mom would laugh,
a sort of strange laugh
too loud and wild-sounding
and sucked at her cigarette
and the funny feeling
I'd get in my stomach.
Yeah, I do.

Not Ready

It took fifty-two years to hear
your voice over the phone.
We spoke once a month for a year.
You lived in San Diego
I was in Vancouver.
During the first call you explained
how you met my mother
at a house party in Harwick.
I was conceived the same night
in a stranger's bed while a fight
broke out in the living room.
Four months later my mother
called to say she was pregnant.
You met my grandfather
for lunch in a tavern on Freeport Road.
You didn't eat. Your hand shook
too much to lift your beer
as he watched you across the table
and deemed you unfit to be a father.
You were free to walk out into
the cold November afternoon
spared the coal mine or steel mill.
After that art school for a term
then a year in prison for drugs
and the long drive across the country
—a violation of your parole—
to a life in California with a wife,
a home and your own business.
You said you weren't ready
to be a father then and hoped
I understood. You kept asking me
to come for a visit but I didn't have time
then time ran out.

Flash Grenades

What's the point of being sick
If you can't miss work? I saw

a cowboy hat on a naked mannequin.
It made me nostalgic for flapjacks

and molasses. My friend sends oblique
insults at me through poetry,

so I'll be more direct. Fuck off
you sub-zero tapeworm. Netflix

proves there's more than enough
emptiness to go around. When I spin

in circles I see Sylvia Plath watching
with a smile and vase of perfect

tulips I could never hope to replicate.
Every fairground freak had a mother

gushing with love like a burst artery.
This living hurtles past like a runaway

train. When the muses
finally decide to transfigure me

I'll blind everyone like a flash grenade
exploding in a waiting room. In the

after-dark we'll hold hands until
the receptionist calls our names.

A Winter's Moon

I'm on the 99 bus when the man
beside me takes off his mask. He drops it
on the floor, covers it with his work boot
squishes it like he's killing a bug
or extinguishing a cigarette. I look through
the tangle of arms and shoulders
to watch gray buildings and traffic
slipping past. Even in the late afternoon
December shadows that fill the bus
I feel the stare of eyes over the fabric patches
covering our faces. I understand
their anger that is fear and feel it too. Afraid
of the poisoned air we breathe
in this jostling passage. A man's face
becomes a dangerous thing
ghostly in the dimming transit:
a winter's moon,
a frightened child,
someone we have lost.

Dirty Snow

I thought they were snowflakes
as I walked to the dental office
to have my tooth pulled. When one landed
on the back of my hand I licked it clean,
a habit I've had since childhood.
But instead of a tasteless, melting
against my tongue, it was bitter
and left a tiny, dark smear on my skin.
I tasted more and each time
the same ashy taste and smear.
I thought maybe the pulsing ache
of my abscessed tooth
was distorting my senses
because pain alters how we know
the world. For why would ashes be falling
from the skies over East Vancouver?
I could see no distant fires
licking at the clouds
or pillars of smoke or hear the wail
of sirens. But now the ashes
fell thick and fast, covering
parked cars and concrete
with a grainy five o'clock shadow.
I saw images behind a glass.
Torn faces smeared with ashes
loomed out of the blackened air
to stumble down debris-strewn streets.
I woke and the pain of the infected tooth
shattered my face as flies buzzed
the bloody drool clotting my pillow;
like flies circling the smashed faces
of a thousand Philistines
Samson slew with the jawbone
of an ass.

A Whole Lot of Nothing

I'm parked by the tracks
and the ruined factory

owned now by pigeons,
rats and the odd drifter.

A whole lot of nothing blares
from cheap speakers

dashboard lights
glow like white windows

of distant skyscrapers
over an empty downtown

or lights of tugboats
working the river at night.

When something becomes
familiar the emptiness

shows through. Or as the cheap
speakers are now saying

It's better to burn out than fade
away. A fired employee burnt down

the roller-skating rink last week
where I had my first kiss thirty

years ago. They said you could see
the fire ten miles downriver.

Yeah, I bet you could. It was
one hell of a kiss.

Tara

I was sitting with my ex-wife Tara
on a curb in Pittsburgh. It was a summer
evening and it had just rained. Her skin
was tanned from many days of sunlight
and it was easy between us. We talked
and laughed and I leaned against her
as she leaned into me. I felt the coolness
of her skin and her eyes the green
of jade and bright as rain. Joy flew
my heart straight and light like an arrow
through the evening air in the shadows
of the huge chestnut trees. I woke up
an old man on a narrow bed
in a small room. I hadn't
spoken to her for years.

PTSD

He kept a knife beside his bed.
Some nights the blade glinted silver
in the light that crept past the edges
of the blinds. Some nights he'd wake
from bad dreams to touch the black handle
to feel he was safe. Some nights
he pushed the dresser over to block
the bedroom door. Those were the worst nights
when he couldn't shut his eyes
because of the shapes blossoming
both in the mind and room's darkness.
When he was married he put the knife
under the bed on his side, but
she would find it and take it away.
Once when she asked him why,
he almost spoke but turned his face
to the wall. That was years ago
now he can sleep alone
with his knife and a barricaded door.

A Thin Thread of Light

I lived on the streets until I hated it.
I stole clothing, food, alcohol
cigarettes to survive. Then I went
from boarding house to boarding house
until I hated them. After that I lived
in basement suites and apartments.
I was evicted often or crept away
at night clutching a garbage bag
of unwashed clothing and books.
I worked minimum wage jobs and drank.
I blacked out, woke up in drunk tanks
to black coffee,
dry toast,
a black eye,
bruised ribs,
a broken nose,
fired again
for failing to show.
I woke up hungover
on a Greyhound bus
as it pulled into the Calgary
station at 6 AM and hitchhiked
back to Vancouver with five dollars
and two flaps of coke in my pockets,
nearly freezing to death on the Crow's Nest
after arguing with a truck driver
who left me on the side of the highway
in a snowstorm. I fought outside bars
with other drunks or college boys
slumming it, rage flying out of me
as fist met bone, the close struggle
as we wrestled to the cement,

to walk away with bloodied knuckles
bruises on my face, adrenaline
shaking my limbs and flooding my mind.
These were things I understood and wanted.
Depression, a huge stone pressing down
upon me, failed suicide attempts,
found and strapped to a gurney,
ambulances wailing to emergency rooms,
my stomach pumped as angry nurses
stared into my waking eyes
dragged back from a blackness
I'd wanted. Psych wards
sedated and locked into white rooms.
And through it all,
poetry; the thinnest thread of light.
Sylvia Plath's red tulips bullying me
back to health in the hospital, Charles Bukowski
drinking and fighting alongside me
in bars and back alleys,
Al Purdy explaining this strange country
while piling sixty-pound bags of plaster mix,
erecting scaffolding on construction sites,
gutting burnt buildings on demo jobs,
my lungs choked with ashes
until I nearly died from an asthma attack.
John Keats whispering nightingale songs
as I coughed with pneumonia,
shaking beneath blankets and curtains
stripped from windows for warmth
because I'd drank away the money
to buy oil for the furnace.
Writing my own lines on scraps of paper,
buying my first typewriter at the Value Village,
clacking away night after night,
page after page of awful poems

no one rightfully wanted to read.
Hauling them around in a briefcase
plucked from a dumpster,
my worthless poems,
my wonderful, worthless poems.
A thin thread of light that led
me here to you.

Brazilian Jiu-Jitsu

Each time I walk off the mats
something else hurts: ankles,
knees, elbows, neck, back
sometimes all of them
at the same time. And that's
not counting real injuries
that require surgery or months
of rest. What am I doing grappling
in pajamas with young men
half my age — bigger, stronger
and faster — who do anything
I can do better? Men who move
with the grace of dancers
the skill of trained killers.
Why do I spend hours stretching
drilling techniques
and studying videos
when I should take up gardening,
write my memoirs,
or spend afternoons drinking coffee
outside cafes with my fellow geezers?
I'm only getting older and slower
until the day my body gives out and I wash
my sweaty pajamas for the last time
and give them away. But sometimes
I forget myself and move
with an ease I don't often possess
and sweep my opponent as his body
becomes light as air
or he catches me in a choke
gently applies pressure
until I tap his arm to submit

which is a kind of pretend death.
Then we smile and get up
to fight again.

My Blue Apartment*

I paid a young woman with stolen money
to paint it before I moved in. A fantasy
of Aegean skies conjured by my illiterate heart
her blue-dipped brush to breed — like the brutal,
beautiful myths I'd read through the night —
songs to sound the fury and mire of my paddler's
veins. Poor singer that I am, blue walls sheltered
in watery womb, a man-shape to breathe cramped air.
As my gilled lungs quivered like a plucked jaw's
harp sounding its one reverberating note
I saw the blue eye stare through blue walls
watching my crawling song. It closed
and walls collapsed like waves
to blot my scanty light. But opened again
and walls were gone and light poured
through my bricked perch above the street
and all of it was blue.

*After reading Russell Thornton's *Answer to Blue*

Stop Being Old

I'm lying on the carpet
in the living room counting
ceiling tiles. Lucy and Marcia
are in the kitchen shout-singing
to a Lizzo song as they mix batter
for a cake:

I do my hair toss
Check my nails
Baby how you feeling
Feeling good as hell.

My back feels like hell
and not the good kind
Lizzo sings about.
Partial sacralization
of the L5 vertebrae
to the sacrum bone
and a Brazilian Jiu-Jitsu
class the day before
have conspired
to put me on the floor
as my lower back muscles
clench up like knotted fists.
I'm counting tiles
to focus my mind
away from the pain.
An explosion
of girlish laughter
and Lucy roars
into the living room
Rodney! Rodney!

She tells me to come
to the kitchen because they're
going to have a dance party.
I say I can't because I've hurt
my back. She tells me it's
my own fault. *How's that?* I
ask. She stares at me
as she scrunches her face
then throws her hands
into the air and shouts
*Stop being old right now,
and come dance with us!*

The Hug

Since she was five
Lucy likes to give me
a hug by positioning me
on one side of the living room.
She retraces her steps
to the opposite side
then turns to charge at me.
When she gets a couple feet
away she launches herself into the air
like a human projectile.
It's more tackle than hug
except I'm expected to remain
standing to catch her. For which she'll
give me a quick squeeze
like a reverse Heimlich manoeuver
and abruptly let go. *There*,
she'll say with a nod of her head
as if she's conferred upon me
an enormous favour.
You can go home now.
But at thirteen it's getting
harder to catch her.
Last week she caught me
flat-footed and I stumbled
backwards onto my ass.
When I held out my hand
for her to help me up
she shook her head
and marched back
across the room.
You need practice, she said
and charged.